THE WINE
QUIZ BOOK

500 Questions and Answers to Test
and Build Your Wine Knowledge

THE WINE
QUIZ BOOK

500 Questions and Answers to Test
and Build Your Wine Knowledge

COMPILED BY

RODDY BUTTON AND MIKE OLIVER

APEX PUBLISHING LTD

First published in 2016 by

Apex Publishing Ltd

12A St. John's Road, Clacton on Sea, Essex, CO15 4BP, United Kingdom

www.apexpublishing.co.uk

British Library Cataloguing-in-Publication Data
A catalogue record for this book
is available from the British Library

ISBN: 978-1-911476-26-9

Typeset in 12pt Palatino Linotype

Production Manager: Chris Cowlin

Publisher's Note:
The views and opinions expressed in this publication are those of the authors and are not necessarily those of Apex Publishing Ltd

CONTENTS

ANSWERS   53

ABOUT THE AUTHORS   73

QUESTIONS

GENERAL WINE QUESTIONS - INTRODUCTION

1. In which decade did Phylloxera start to decimate the grapes in French vineyards – 1860s, 1870s, 1880s?

2. How many different grape varieties are there in the world – 3,000, 5,000, 8,000+?

3. In which country is the grape Zinfandel most commonly found?

4. In which country is Touriga Nacional mainly grown?

5. Which grape variety is the most grown in the world?

6. Which country now produces the most Malbec?

7. Which grape has the thickest skin – Cabernet Sauvignon or Pinot Noir?

8. Which grape makes wine that sometimes has the aroma of diesel or petrol?

9. What is a wine barrel-maker called?

10. Which country produces the wine 'Pingus'?

MATCH THESE FAMOUS WINES OF THE NEW WORLD WITH THEIR COUNTRY/WINE AREA

11.	Isabel Estate	USA/Napa Valley
12.	Chateau St. Michelle	Canada/Ontario
13.	Chateau Changyu-Castel	India/Narayangaon
14.	Leeuwin Estate	Mexico/Baja California
15.	Gillmore Estate	USA/Washington State
16.	Kanonkop Estate	China/Shandong
17.	Vineland Estate	New Zealand/Marlborough
18.	Chateau Indage	Chile/Maule
19.	Chateau Camou	Australia/Margaret River
20.	Chateau Montelena	South Africa/ Stellenbosch

MATCH THESE FAMOUS WINES OF EUROPE AND THE MIDDLE EAST WITH THEIR COUNTRY/WINE AREA

21.	Denbies Estate	Lebanon/Bekaa Valley
22.	Chateau Bezanec	Bulgaria
23.	Chateau Carras	Austria/Kamptal
24.	Chateau Maison Blanche	Germany/Baden
25.	Chateau Musar	England/Surrey
26.	Schloss Gobelsberg Estate	Israel
27.	Dr Heger Estate	Switzerland
28.	Chateau St. Andre	Greece/Macedonia
29.	Chateau de Val	Croatia
30.	Chateau Golan	Hungary/Eger

ANAGRAMS – WELL KNOWN WINE BRANDS

31.   see crack job

32.   ben castrate tot

33.   to a document

34.   damn lines

35.   send flop

ANAGRAMS – WELL KNOWN CHAMPAGNES

36.   men drooping

37.   noble girl

38.   ignite tart

39.   hand on tome etc

40.   due rosier role

WINES OF FRANCE - Part 1

41. From which grape is Sancerre made?

42. Up to how many different grape varieties is Chateauneuf du Pape made?

43. Brut champagne can be made from red grapes – True or False?

44. Which is the only red grape grown with AOC status in the Loire Valley?

45. What was Winston Churchill's favourite champagne?

46. From which wine region does Volnay come?

47. In which region would you find Vin de Pays d'Oc?

48. Which champagne featured in the TV series Absolutely Fabulous?

49. From which region does Chateau Cheval Blanc come?

50. From which grape is Chablis made?

WINES OF FRANCE - Part 2

51.   Which famous monk was reputed to have put the bubbles in champagne?

52.   Which grape is used to produce Beaujolais?

53.   Name 2 of the 3 main grapes used to make champagne?

54.   Which is the main white grape variety grown in the middle Loire?

55.   What does a 'remueur' do?

56.   In what year was the official classification of Classed Growth Bordeaux wines?

57.   Which champagne was the favourite of Tsar Nicholas II of Russia?

58.   How many Beaujolais crus are there?

59.   Near which river is Hermitage wine produced?

60.   What is the most planted grape in champagne?

WINES OF FRANCE - Part 3

61. In which area of Bordeaux is Chateau Lafite produced?

62. What are the 2 main towns in the champagne region?

63. Which wine region has traditionally put the grape variety on the front label?

64. In which wine region can the town of Riquewihr be found?

65. Which champagne is often called 'The Widow'?

66. Which of these is a white burgundy – Pouilly Fumé or Pouilly Fuissé?

67. Which wine is made from the Melon de Bourgogne grape?

68. What type of soil is mainly found in the champagne region?

69. Alsace is mainly known for its white wine, but which red grape variety is most commonly grown there?

70. Which wine is produced in the highest volume in the Loire Valley?

WINES OF FRANCE - Part 4

71.   Roughly how many champagne growers are there in the champagne region – 9,000, 14,000, 19,000?

72.   Name 1 of the 4 main wines from the Cote Chalonnaise?

73.   In the champagne region what is an RM (Recoltant Manipulant)?

74.   In which wine region is Cabernet Sauvignon grown – Burgundy or Bordeaux?

75.   From which wine region does Sancerre come?

76.   What is the remuage process in champagne making?

77.   Gamay is the main grape variety grown in which wine region?

78.   Blanc de Blanc champagne can be made from both red and white grapes – True or False?

79.   In which wine region is the city of Dijon?

80.   Which one of these grapes is often used in the champagne region – Pinot Blanc, Pinot Meunier, Pinot Gris?

WINES OF FRANCE - Part 5

81.   In which wine region is Gewurztraminer most commonly found?

82.   In which region can the dessert wine Chateau d'Yquem be found?

83.   Which colour wine is Provence most famous for?

84.   Which alcohol content is champagne most likely to be – 10.5%, 12.5%, 14.5%?

85.   Which town is Burgundy's wine capital?

86.   Which of these is the largest wine producing region in France – Languedoc-Roussillon, Bordeaux, Rhone Valley?

87.   Which champagne house does not carry out malolactic fermentation in order to keep the wine "razor sharp"?

88.   Which Burgundy town hosts the annual charity Hospices wine auction?

89.   Name 5 of the Beaujolais Crus?

90.   From which principal grape variety is Cahors made?

MATCH THESE TOP FRENCH CHATEAUX WITH THEIR WINE/VINEYARD AREAS – Part 1

91.	Chateau Petrus	Northern Rhone
92.	Chateau des Jacques	Jura/Vin Jaune
93.	Chateau Grillet	Burgundy/ Cote de Beaune
94.	Chateau d'Yquem	Beaujolais/ Moulin-a-Vent
95.	Chateaud'Ampuis	Bordeaux/Medoc
96.	Chateau de Pommard	Bordeaux/Pomerol
97.	Chateau de la Grille	Bordeaux/ Pessac Leognan/Graves
98.	Chateau Haut Brion	Bordeaux/Sauternes
99.	Chateau Lafite	Northern Rhone/ Cote Rotie
100.	Chateau Chalon	Loire/Chinon

MATCH THESE FRENCH WINES WITH THEIR WINE/VINEYARD AREAS – Part 2

101. Bouzy Rouge   Languedoc/Herault

102. Bouvet-Ladubay   Rhone North/
                               Hermitage

103. Vieux Telegraphe   Champagne/
                               Pinot area

104. Mas de Daumas Gassac   Alsace

105. Clos de Gamot   Cote Chalonnaise

106. Trimbach
     Vendage Tardive   Champagne/Epernay

107. Chapoutier L'Ermite   Cahors

108. Dom Perignon   Burgundy/
                               Cote de Nuits

109. Domaine de la   Rhone South/
     Romanee Conti   Chateauneuf du Pape

110. Faiveley Mercurey   Loire/ Saumur

ANAGRAMS - FRANCE

French Grape Varieties

111. canny hoard

112. no no rip it

113. be calm

114. my aga

115. rigs line

French Wines

116. neat users

117. change map

118. tape up a deaf eunuch

119. usual term

120. elevators

WINES OF ITALY – Part 1

121. In which region is Chianti produced?

122. Which of these grape varieties is Italian –
      Torrontes, Shiraz, Sangiovese?

123. Name a grape beginning with the letter 'B' from
      the Piedmont region?

124. From which grape variety is Barolo made?

125. What is the most southerly wine-growing region
      in mainland Italy?

126. What is an Amarone?

127. Castello Banfi, in Montalcino, is owned and run
      by a family from which country ?

128. When was the famous Florentine house of
      Antinori founded – 1385, 1485, 1585?

129. In which region was the very first Italian school
      for wine growing and oenology created in 1885 –
      Piedmont, Tuscany, Veneto?

130. Does Italy produce more red wine or white wine?

WINES OF ITALY – Part 2

131.   What high quality wines are produced in Valdobbiadene?

132.   What is the closest wine growing region to Rome?

133.   What is the classic Umbrian white wine called?

134.   What is the symbol/emblem found on the neck of Chianti Classico bottles?

135.   What is the oldest wine estate in Piedmont?

136.   On the banks of which lake are Valpolicella wine grapes grown?

137.   Which wine is still regarded as Italy's king of wines?

138.   Which wine region is the most northerly in Italy, and forms part of the southern tip of Austria's Tyrol?

139.   What is the name of the wine from Montefiascone near Rome which Hugh Johnson called "the dullest white wine with the strangest name in the world"?

140.   From which grape variety is Prosecco made?

MATCH FAMOUS ITALIAN WINES WITH THEIR DOC AREAS

141.	Frascati	Puglia
142.	Barolo	Tuscany
143.	Orvieto	Veneto
144.	Greco di Tufo	Sardinia
145.	Copertino	Le Marche
146.	Chianti	Piedmont
147.	Valpolicella	Roma/Lazio
148.	Rosso Piceno	Umbria
149.	Vermentino di Gallura	Sicily
150.	Etna Rosso	Campania

ANAGRAMS – ITALY

Italian Grape Varieties

151. bear bra

152. core cops

153. old octet

154. invent more

155. clean up motion

Italian Wines

156. lob oar

157. fair acts

158. a sober crab

159. chain it

160. a giant rat

WINES OF SPAIN – Part 1

161. What is the principal grape used to make red Rioja?

162. What is Spanish sparkling wine commonly known as?

163. Toro wine is produced in the south of Spain, True or False?

164. The Ribera del Duero wine region is in the north of Spain, True or False?

165. Is a wine labelled Tinto red or white?

166. Which well-known Spanish city is closest to the wine region of Priorat?

167. Which region is best known for producing Albariño?

168. For which white wine is the Rueda region well-known?

169. The grape variety Grenache is known by a different name. What is it?

170. From which region does Vega Sicilia come?

WINES OF SPAIN – Part 2

171. What is the name of Spain's largest wine region?

172. The River Ebro runs through which Spanish wine region?

173. What is the driest form of sherry called?

174. What percentage of Rioja wine is white?

175. What is Spain's smallest wine region called?

176. Spain's best known wine family, Torres, is based in which wine region?

177. Which is the oldest bodega in Rioja?

178. Which Cava House produces over 60% of all Cava?

179. Which is the most northerly DO wine region; it's in the east of Spain?

180. In making sherry, what is the system of topping up casks with older sherry called?

ANAGRAMS – SPAIN

Spanish Grape Varieties

181.   all time porn

182.   baronial

183.   in a crane

184.   not smaller

185.   parade all

Spanish Wine Regions

186.   airport

187.   deride labourer

188.   deepens

189.   six arabias

190.   on to moans

WINES OF NEW ZEALAND – Part 1

191. Which grape variety is grown the most in New Zealand?

192. What is the name of the wine region situated to the west of Marlborough?

193. The wine producer 'Mud House' is located on New Zealand's North Island – True or False?

194. What is the name of New Zealand's southernmost wine region?

195. Which wine area on the South Island has the same name as a well-known Kent town?

196. Which Austrian white grape variety is also grown in New Zealand?

197. A widely planted grape variety in New Zealand also produces the French wines of Sancerre and Pouilly Fumé – what is it called?

198. Which produces the most wine – North Island or South Island?

199. Which global company now owns the famous Cloudy Bay?

200. Which wine growing region of New Zealand produces the most Merlot?

WINES OF NEW ZEALAND – Part 2

201. Which is the largest wine growing area (volume and size) in New Zealand?

202. Actor Sam Neill produces top Pinot Noir in Central Otago. What is the winery's name?

203. Which giant French company currently owns and produces around 40% of New Zealand wines?

204. What proportion of the world's wine crop does New Zealand currently produce – 0.5%, 1.5%, 2.5%?

205. In the year 2000 NZ produced fewer than 7 million cases of wine, what had this expanded to by 2015 – 15 million, 20 million, 30 million?

206. Approximately how many wineries are there in New Zealand?

207. Which is the fastest growing wine region?

208. Which country imports the most NZ wine?

209. What percentage of wines are exported - 25%, 50%, 75%?

210. Which winery has won the most wine awards over the past 30 years?

ANAGRAMS – NEW ZEALAND

New Zealand Wine Regions

211.   homo burglar

212.   sobering

213.   a shaky web

214.   anal duck

215.   nectar to a log

New Zealand Wine Producers

216.   mail a rival

217.   rat again

218.   destroying

219.   cast neat jokes

220.   a lot of nerd

WINES OF CHILE

221. Which of these wine regions is the most southerly – Maipo, Limari, Bio Bio?

222. What is the most widely grown grape variety in Chile?

223. Which Chilean grape variety used to be confused with Merlot?

224. Which famous Spanish wine family own extensive vineyards in Chile?

225. Los Vascos winery is owned by which famous First Growth property in Bordeaux?

226. Which wine region near Santiago has the hottest climate?

227. There were 12 wineries in Chile in 1995. Approximately how many were there in 2015 – 240, 340 , 440?

228. What is special about Chilean grapevines and root stock?

229. Chile is now in the top 10 exporters of wine by value in the world, but in what position – 4th, 7th, 9th?

230. Which Chilean winery is not only the largest in Chile, but also in the whole of South America?

WINES OF ARGENTINA

231.   What is the red grape variety that Argentina is most famous for?

232.   When is the grape harvest time in Argentina – Jan/Feb, Mar/Apr, May/Jun?

233.   Is Bonarda a white or red grape?

234.   When were the first vineyards planted in Argentina; 1557, 1657, 1757?

235.   What is the largest wine growing area in Argentina?

236.   In Patagonia what are the southernmost planted vineyards in the Americas – Bodegas Esmerelda, Bodegas Weinert, Bodegas Trapiche?

237.   Which is the only Austrian owned Bodega in Argentina – Etchart, Norton, Weinert?

238.   Which white grape grown extensively in Argentina has floral, muscat-like aromas and a spicy note?

239.   Approximately how many separate wineries (wine companies) are there in Argentina – 900, 1200, 1500?

240.   What is the oldest current winery in Argentina, at over 180 years old – Colome, Lagarde, Valentin Bianchi?

ANAGRAMS – SOUTH AMERICA

South American Grape Varieties

241. career men

242. stern root

243. ban road

244. beat robin

245. ant tan

Argentinian and Chilean Wine Regions

246. a goat pain

247. travel cleanly

248. sat an onion

249. atlas

250. a mule

WINES OF GERMANY – Part 1

251. What does QmP stand for on a German wine label?

252. What is the name of a wine that is made from grapes picked when they are frozen?

253. In terms of quality level and sweetness, what is the next style in the sequence – Kabinett, Spatlese, ……..?

254. If a German wine is described as Trocken, is it dry or sweet?

255. Which well known grape variety is called Spätburgunder in Germany?

256. What do the letters TBA mean when referring to a very high quality wine?

257. Name either of the 2 main tributaries of the Mosel river?

258. What is the name of Germany's southernmost wine region?

259. What is the name of the flat, round-bellied bottle used in the Franken region?

260. Three regions are especially known for their production of red wine, name one?

WINES OF GERMANY – Part 2

261. Which country imports and drinks the most German wine – USA, Netherlands, UK?

262. Plantings of red grapes now account for approximately what percentage of Germany's vineyards – 15%, 25%, 35%?

263. Which is the least sweet of these top QmP wines – Auslese, Kabinett, Spatlese?

264. Which grape variety is the most widely planted in Germany?

265. Glock in Nierstein is reputed to be the oldest vineyard in Germany. When did it start – 642AD, 742AD, 842AD?

266. Trockenbeerenauslese is Germany's sweetest and most expensive category of German wine. What is its minimum alcohol content – 5.5%, 7.5%, 9.5%?

267. What does Bereich or Grosslage on a German wine label mean – made from inferior grapes, a blend from different regions, produced from a blend of different vintages?

268. Which river connects the wine towns of Trier, Piesport and Bernkastel?

269. What was the Pfaltz wine region called in English?

270. Which wine area produces the most wine? Rheingau, Rheinhessen, Pfalz?

ANAGRAMS – GERMANY

German Grape Varieties

271.   red fondler

272.   ring lies

273.   see cherub

274.   sure ego trip

275.   vary lens

German Wine Towns

276.   poets rip

277.   hide demise

278.   of neck

279.   thin termite

280.   tell evil

WINES OF U.S.A. – CALIFORNIA – Part 1

281. When were vineyards first planted in California – 1648, 1769, 1833?

282. About how many wineries are there in California – 2,700, 3,700, 4,700?

283. What is the largest wine growing area in California – Napa Valley, Sonoma, Central Valley?

284. Which colour grape is grown the most in California, red or white?

285. Which Californian wine-maker has a joint venture with Chateau Mouton Rothschild to make Opus One?

286. How many AVAs (American Viticultural Areas) are there in California – 50, 80, 100?

287. What is said to be the native variety of grape in California?

288. What percentage of a grape has to be in a bottle in order to call it by the grape name on the front label e.g. Chardonnay, Cabernet Sauvignon etc – 85%, 95%, 100%?

289. What percentage of USA wine is produced in California – 60%, 80%, 90%?

290. Which is California's most planted grape variety – Cabernet Sauvignon, Chardonnay, Merlot?

WINES OF U.S.A. – CALIFORNIA – Part 2

291. Which famous film director (e.g. The Godfather) now makes 'Rubicon' wine in Napa Valley?

292. Which Californian red wine beat the French in the 'Judgement of Paris' competition in 1976?

293. Which is the largest wine company in California?

294. Name 2 of the 4 French Champagne Houses making Californian sparkling wine?

295. The Oscar winning 'Sideways' film was a trip around which wine area?

296. Which 'County' is California's most northerly wine growing outpost?

297. What % volume of all Californian wine comes from Napa Valley - 5%, 10%, 15%?

298. California is now the World's 4th, 5th or 6th largest wine producer by value?

299. Name the Port like wine, using the same grape varieties, made by Quady?

300. What was President Obama's favourite Californian white wine?

ANAGRAMS – U.S.A. – CALIFORNIA

Californian Wine Valleys

301. a rascal ant

302. o no sam

303. dane

304. a zany nest

305. cry derek

Californian Wine Producers

306. green rib

307. non nobody

308. steal gaps

309. I am not a club

310. name neat cute halo

WINES OF PORTUGAL

311.   What is the sweet wine, just south of Lisbon and made from Muscat grapes?

312.   Two wine producing regions are UNESCO World Heritage Sites - name one?

313.   What is the slightly prickly and very acid white wine from the Minho Region?

314.   About how many DOC wine areas are there - 20, 30, 40?

315.   Name the English pop singer who owns a bodega producing Vida Nova wines?

316.   What is the name of the world's best selling medium dry rosé?

317.   What is the word for a sparkling wine put on labels?

318.   Which fortified wine is cooked using the Estufa Process?

319.   Which wine area of Ramisco grapes is grown on extensive sand dunes?

320.   Which is the oldest Port House founded in 1638 - Kopke, Taylor's, Warre's?

ANAGRAMS – PORTUGAL

Port Producers

321.   quit on a vandal

322.   curb conk

323.   lays rot

324.   on faces

325.   dans mean

Portuguese DOC Wines

326.   seal cub

327.   or duo

328.   arid arab

329.   late bus

330.   ado

WINES OF SOUTH AFRICA

331.   What % of South African Wine is White - 35%,
        55%, 65%?

332.   Founded in 1918, what was the state owned wine
        company called?

333.   What was Napoleon's death bed wine, his
        favourite dessert wine?

334.   Which pioneer winery in Walkers Bay first
        produced "Burgundian" whites & reds?

335.   Which country imports more S A bottles of wine
        than any other?

336.   Name the famous golfer who jointly owns a
        prestige winery?

337.   What is the name of the unique red grape, created
        in S A in 1925?

338.   Name Charles Back's "homage" to Cote du Rhone
        wines. It's now an international brand?

339.   Which winery has the Queen stayed at, and is a
        favourite of Buckingham Palace?

340.   What is the widest planted grape variety in
        volume acreage?

ANAGRAMS – SOUTH AFRICA

South African Wine Regions

341.   not satanic

342.   shell ten cobs

343.   harsh of neck

344.   torn robes

345.   bar weakly

South African Wine Producers

346.   books freely

347.   regret buns

348.   rest mule

349.   green bets

350.   hate elm

WINES OF AUSTRALIA – Part 1

351.   Name the oldest Australian winery, planted in 1828 - Reynella, Wyndham, Yalumba?

352.   Which country imports the most Australian wine – USA, Canada, UK?

353.   Name the grape which accounts for 45% of all vines planted in Australia?

354.   Which wine has Hugh Johnson called "the only First Growth in the Southern Hemisphere"?

355.   In which wine region is the Tamar valley, producing top Pinot Noirs & sparklers?

356.   Which huge winery in the Barossa Valley has an Eaglehawk on its label?

357.   Name the Brown Brothers wine that is similar to a good Beaujolais?

358.   Which State produces the most wine - South Australia, Victoria, Western Australia?

359.   The founder of the Australian Wine Bureau also wrote the first Encyclopedia of Australian Wine. Who is he?

360.   The Art Series is produced by which Margaret River Winery?

WINES OF AUSTRALIA – Part 2

361. Which country has the fastest growing consumption levels of Australian wine - USA, China, UK?

362. Which champagne House makes Green Point in the Yarra Valley?

363. Approximately how many wineries are currently producing wine – 2,000, 2,500, 3,000?

364. In which wine area are both Yalumba and Grant Burge based?

365. Which is the most planted white grape variety?

366. On average how many million bottles are produced per year - 1,000, 1,500, 2,000?

367. Who, as "the father of Australian wine", brought the first cuttings from Europe in 1820 - James Busby, Jim Barry, John Parker?

368. Which global wine company owns Wolf Blass, Penfolds and Lindemans - Fosters, Constellation, Saab-Miller?

369. What is Tasmania's most planted grape variety?

370. Who produces and edits the annual Australian Wine Companion - Clive Hartley, James Halliday, Len Evans?

ANAGRAMS – AUSTRALIA

Australian Wine Regions

371.   hell aids ideal

372.   a raw corona

373.   lone egg

374.   e g hurl tern

375.   rival nerd

Australian Wine Producers

376.   sore nit

377.   lobs flaws

378.   on bored wok

379.   a bum lay

380.   pat a mule

WINES OF ENGLAND

381. Which English sparkling wine has been served at Buckingham Palace and has beaten champagnes in tasting competitions?

382. Approximately how many bottles of English wine were produced in 2015 – 3 million, 4 million, 5 million?

383. Which is the largest vineyard in England?

384. Camel Valley, one of the best vineyards in England, is in which county?

385. Which of these is an English Wine – Three Paddocks, Stanlake Park, Parra Farm?

386. Ryedale is the most northerly vineyard producing commercially in England. What is the nearest city to it – Leicester, Sheffield, York?

387. The largest vineyard in Gloucestershire has a singing reference in its name. What is it called?

388. Approximately what proportion of English wine is red – 10%, 20%, 30%?

389. According to the English Wine Producers Association, how many white grape varieties are used in wine-making in England – 12, 17, 22?

390. When were the first vineyards planted in England – 43AD, 143AD, 343AD?

ANAGRAMS – ENGLAND

English Wine Producers

391. ben dies

392. took barmy bet

393. tiny ember

394. leave calmly

395. richest hero

English Wine Grape Varieties

396. cash cub

397. scorn her bug

398. render fold

399. cleans v ably

400. or nod

WINES OF AUSTRIA / HUNGARY / GREECE

401. What is Austria's white flagship grape covering around 37% of vineyards?

402. Does Blaufrankisch produce a white or red wine?

403. About what percentage of Austrian wines are exported - 10%, 25%, 40%?

404. The best sweet Botrytis dessert wines come from which Austrian wine region?

405. What is Hungarian Bulls Blood now called?

406. What is the sweet wine from Hungary, sweetness measured in Puttonyos?

407. Most Hungarian white wine comes from wine regions around Europe's largest lake; what is the lake called?

408. Which volcanic island, north of Crete, now produces some of the best dry and sweet white wines in Greece?

409. What is the name of the oldest producer of fine wines in Greece?

410. What Greek white wine has pine resin added?

ANAGRAMS – AUSTRIA

Austrian Wine Regions

411. wine

412. lets mark

413. grub led nan

414. raw mag

415. map talk

Austrian Grape Varieties

416. tell unerring rev

417. backlash if run

418. ring lies

419. resultant

420. we get liz

HISTORY OF WINE

421. Approximately how many years BC was wine first used as a beverage – 5k-6k BC, 3k-4k BC, 1k-2k BC?

422. In which country have the oldest remnants of wine been discovered – Lebanon, Iraq, Iran?

423. When was the glass bottle introduced – 16th Century, 17th Century, 18th Century?

424. Corks were first introduced as stoppers for wine enclosures in which Century?

425. In which decade of the 20th Century was the Appellation d'Origine Controlee system introduced in France?

426. Which vintage in Bordeaux did American wine expert Robert Parker call "superb", in opposition to other experts, which got him worldwide attention?

427. When was méthode champenoise, with a 2nd fermentation invented - 1662, 1762, 1862?

428. Which 2 wines imported into England in the 1600s were known as Claret and Sack?

429. Which wine, often one of the 3 most expensive wines in the world, had its first vintage made in 1979?

430. Stelvin screw caps, now on over 5 billion bottles a year, was invented in which country?

WINE GROWING and WINE MAKING

431.   Which are the two main months for pruning vines in the northern hemisphere – Jan/Feb, Mar/Apr, May/Jun?

432.   Around what age is a vine when its yields start declining – 25 to 30 years, 35 to 40 years, 45 to 50 years?

433.   What does 'terroir' mean?

434.   What temperature range is best for the fermentation of white wines - 16-21C, 22-26C, or 27-30C?

435.   What is the purpose of using egg whites in the process of wine making?

436.   What is 'must'?

437.   On average, how many grapes go into a bottle of wine – 300, 600, 900?

438.   Which tight grained French oak is judged to be best for maturing fine Bordeaux wines - Vosges, Troncais or Limousin?

439.   How many years does a Gran Reserva Rioja stay in barrel before bottling?

440.   How many bottles of Bordeaux wine does a barrique barrel hold – 240, 300, 360?

WINE TASTING

441. How many different smells are human beings apparently able to distinguish – 1,000, 5,000, 10,000 plus?

442. What are the four basic taste sensations in the mouth?

443. What is the purpose of tasting a wine in a restaurant before it's poured?

444. If a wine smells and tastes of grass, nettles and asparagus, with zingy lime zest, what grape is it made from?

445. What is wrong with a wine when it's corked?

446. Who is the most famous American wine taster, who influences the taste and prices of some fine Bordeaux wines, as well as certain wines from other countries, and who introduced a 100 points scoring system for wines?

447. Which grape makes wine that is quite tannic when young, and takes oak maturity well to age into a character of herby, pencil-case and blackcurrant aroma?

448. What do the 'legs' left on the inside of a wine glass when swirled indicate – high alcohol content, a full heavy wine, good quality?

449. Which delicate thin-skinned grape produces light red wines with a strawberry aroma and sometimes a smell of plastic?

450. When tasting wine what does a 'long finish' mean?

FAMOUS PEOPLE/FAMOUS WINES – Part 1

451. What was James Bond's favourite champagne in later books and films?

452. Which red wine was most often seen on Tony Soprano's dinner table – Barolo, Chianti Ruffino, Brunello?

453. Who, in his novel based on Long Island, wrote of how the 19 year old Daisy got drunk on Sauternes, regretting his decision to get married to her?

454. Which champagne did Winston Churchill name one of his race horses after?

455. In the film 'Sideways' what was Miles' favourite grape variety?

456. What was Marilyn Monroe's favourite champagne?

457. Which famous early English author and poet was the son of a top wine merchant and deputy to the king's butler – Geoffrey Chaucer, Christopher Marlow, William Shakespeare?

458. What is the current value of the Government's wine stock in the cellars at Westminster - £1million, £2million, £3million?

459. Chambertin was the favourite red wine of which emperor?

460. Which English sparkling wine was served at Buckingham Palace for President Obama's state banquet in 2011?

FAMOUS PEOPLE/FAMOUS WINES – Part 2

461.   Which New Zealand actor owns a top Pinot Noir winery in Central Otago?

462.   Name the Supermarket whose wines are stocked extensively in Buckingham Palace cellars?

463.   Name the original Celebrity Chef whose autobiography is "Stirred but not Shaken"?

464.   Name the very expensive bottle of wine which was bought by Forbes for $160,000?

465.   What was Saddam Hussein's favourite wine? His palaces' cellars were filled with it - Chablis, Chianti or Mateus Rosé?

466.   Hannibal Lecter bought this sweet wine for Clarice Starling's 33rd birthday?

467.   What was President Obama's favourite sparkling wine - Krug, Roederer Estate, Graham Beck's?

468.   Where does the house white of Gordon Ramsey's restaurants for over 10 years come from?

469.   Wine lover Johnny Depp's favourite everyday red is – Ch. Calon-Segur, Ch. Petrus, Ch. Canon?

470.   Which singer's father owns the Ciccone vineyard in Michegan USA?

FAMOUS WINE QUOTES — Part 1

471. When doing what did Dom Perignon say "I am drinking the stars"?

472. Which English playwright wrote "I pray you do not fall in love with me, for I am falser than vows made in wine"?

473. Which Victorian English author wrote "Fan the flames of hilarity with the wings of friendship, and pass the rosy wine"?

474. Who said "Penicillin cures, but wine makes people happy"?

475. Who in his prologue wrote "Strong was the wine and pleasant to each guest, we drank and then to rest went everyone"?

476. Who said "In victory you deserve champagne, in defeat you need it"?

477. Who said to Mae West "Once in the wilds of Afghanistan, I lost my corkscrew and we were forced to live on nothing but food and water for days"?

478. Who said "Wine makes daily living easier, less hurried, with fewer tensions and more tolerance" – Thomas Jefferson, George Washington, Benjamin Franklin?

479. During a film, which actor drank Mumm Cordon Rouge champagne in his flat in Paris with his girlfriend, just before the Germans arrived, and said "Here's looking at you kid"?

480. Which theologist said "He who loves not wine, women and song remains a fool his whole life long" – Martin Luther, Thomas Cramner, John Calvin?

FAMOUS WINE QUOTES — Part 2

481. In which book is this quote "Go eat your food with gladness, and drink your wine with a joyful heart, for it is now that God favours what you do"?

482. Which author said "What is better than to sit at the end of the day and drink wine with friends, or substitutes for friends"?

483. Who said "Wine improves with age, the older I get the better I like it"?

484. Which U.S. Statesman said "I live temperately, I double the doctor's recommendation of a glass and a half of wine each day, and even treble it with a friend"?

485. Who said "This is one of the disadvantages of wine, it makes man mistake words for thought" – Samuel Butler, Samuel Johnson, Samuel Pepys?

486. From which film is this quote "Oh Jesus, don't ask questions like that up in wine country, they'll think you're some kind of dumbshit, OK"?

487. Who said "In wine there is health ("in vino sanitas") – Julius Caesar, Pliny the Elder, Emperor Claudius?

488. Who said "When I put my nose in a glass it's like tunnel vision, I move into another world where everything around me is just gone, and every bit of energy is focused on that wine" – Jancis Robinson, Robert Parker, Hugh Johnson?

489. Which great British actor and drinker said "I'm only drinking white wine because I'm on a diet and I don't eat"?

490. Which great American writer said "Always do sober, what you said you'd do drunk.
That will teach you to keep your mouth shut"?

GENERAL WINE QUESTIONS – Finale

491. Name 3 of the 5 first growth Bordeaux red wines under the 1855 Classification?

492. There are vineyards in Wales – True or False?

493. In which colour glass bottle does Germany's Mosel wine normally come?

494. Which wine goes best with seared or grilled salmon – Red, White, Rosé, Any of these?

495. Which colour Brothers is a well-known Australian wine producer?

496. Rioja is always red – True or False?

497. Which county in England is becoming increasingly famous for producing top quality sparkling wine?

498. Which wine do the French recommend you drink with Foie Gras?

499. 1965 was a great vintage in Bordeaux – True or False?

500. Which more familiar grape variety is called Weissburgunder in Germany?

ANSWERS

GENERAL WINE QUESTIONS - INTRODUCTION
1. 1860's
2. 8,000+
3. USA
4. Portugal
5. Cabernet Sauvignon
6. Argentina
7. Cabernet Sauvignon
8. Riesling
9. Cooper
10. Spain (in Ribera del Duero)

MATCH THESE FAMOUS WINES OF THE NEW WORLD WITH THEIR COUNTRY/WINE AREA

11.	Isabel Estate	New Zealand/Marlborough
12.	Chateau St. Michelle	USA/Washington State
13.	Chateau Changyu-Castel	China/Shandong
14.	Leeuwin Estate	Australia/Margaret River
15.	Gillmore Estate	Chile/Maule
16.	Kanonkop Estate	South Africa/Stellenbosch
17.	Vineland Estate	Canada/Ontario
18.	Chateau Indage	India/Narayangaon
19.	Chateau Camou	Mexico/Baja California
20.	Chateau Montelena	USA/Napa Valley

MATCH THESE FAMOUS WINES OF EUROPE AND THE MIDDLE EAST WITH THEIR COUNTRY/WINE AREA

21.	Denbies Estate	England/Surrey
22.	Chateau Bezanec	Croatia
23.	Chateau Carras	Greece/Macedonia
24.	Chateau Maison Blanche	Switzerland
25.	Chateau Musar	Lebanon/Bekaa Valley
26.	Schloss Gobelsberg Estate	Austria/Kamptal
27.	Dr Heger Estate	Germany/Baden
28.	Chateau St. Andre	Hungary/Eger
29.	Chateau de Val	Bulgaria
30.	Chateau Golan	Israel

ANAGRAMS – WELL KNOWN WINE BRANDS

31. Jacobs Creek
32. Brancott Estate
33. Mouton Cadet
34. Lindemans
35. Penfolds

ANAGRAMS – WELL KNOWN CHAMPAGNES

36. Dom Perignon
37. Bollinger
38. Taittinger
39. Moet et Chandon
40. Louis Roederer

WINES OF FRANCE – Part 1

41. White = Sauvignon Blanc; Rose/Red = Pinot Noir
42. 13, but mainly Grenache,Syrah and Mourvedre
43. True
44. Cabernet Franc
45. Pol Roger
46. Burgundy; Cote de Beaune
47. Languedoc-Roussillon
48. Bollinger - "Bolly"
49. Bordeaux – St Emilion
50. Chardonnay

WINES OF FRANCE – Part 2

51. Dom Perignon
52. Gamay
53. Chardonnay, Pinot Noir, Pinot Meunier
54. Chenin Blanc
55. Riddle champagne bottles to get lees to the cork
56. 1855
57. Cristal from Roederer
58. 10
59. Rhone
60. Pinot Noir

WINES OF FRANCE – Part 3

61. Pauillac
62. Reims and Epernay
63. Alsace
64. Alsace
65. Veuve Clicquot
66. Pouilly Fuissé
67. Muscadet
68. Chalk
69. Pinot Noir
70. Muscadet

WINES OF FRANCE – Part 4

71. 19,000
72. Givry, Mercurey, Montagny, Rully
73. A champagne House that buys in grapes as well as growing their own
74. Bordeaux
75. Loire
76. Manipulating bottles to move sediment onto the corks ready for disgorgement.
77. Beaujolais
78. False
79. Burgundy
80. Pinot Meunier

WINES OF FRANCE – Part 5

81. Alsace
82. Bordeaux (Sauternes)
83. Rosé
84. 12.5%
85. Beaune
86. Languedoc-Roussillon
87. Lanson
88. Beaune
89. Brouilly, Chenas, Chiroubles, Cote de Brouilly, Fleurie, Julienas, Morgon, Moulin-a-Vent, Regnie, St Amour
90. Malbec

MATCH THESE TOP FRENCH CHATEAUX WITH THEIR WINE/VINEYARD AREAS – PART 1

91.	Chateau Petrus	Bordeaux/Pomerol
92.	Chateau des Jacques	Beaujolais/Moulin-a-Vent
93.	Chateau Grillet	Northern Rhone
94.	Chateau d'Yquem	Bordeaux/Sauternes
95.	Chateau d'Ampuis	Northern Rhone/Cote Rotie
96.	Chateau de Pommard	Burgundy/Cote de Beaune
97.	Chateau de la Grille	Loire/Chinon
98.	Chateau Haut Brion	Bordeaux/Pessac Leognan/Graves
99.	Chateau Lafite	Bordeaux/Medoc
100.	Chateau Chalon	Jura/Vin Jaune

MATCH THESE FRENCH WINES WITH THEIR WINE/VINEYARD AREAS – PART 2

101.	Bouzy Rouge	Champagne/Pinot area
102.	Bouvet-Ladubay	Loire/Saumur
103.	Vieux Telegraphe	Rhone South/Chateauneuf du Pape
104.	Mas de Daumas Gassac	Languedoc/Herault
105.	Clos de Gamot	Cahors
106.	Trimbach Vendage Tardive	Alsace
107.	Chapoutier L'Ermite	Rhone North/Hermitage
108.	Dom Perignon	Champagne/Epernay
109.	Domaine de la Romanee Conti	Burgundy/Cote de Nuits
110.	Faiveley Mercurey	Cote Chalonnaise

ANAGRAMS - FRANCE

French Grape Varieties

111. Chardonnay
112. Pinot Noir
113. Malbec
114. Gamay
115. Riesling

French Wines

116. Sauternes
117. Champagne
118. Chateauneuf du Pape

119.   Meursault
120.   Tavel Rose

WINES OF ITALY – Part 1
121.   Tuscany
122.   Sangiovese
123.   Barbera, Bonarda, Brachetta
124.   Nebbiolo
125.   Calabria
126.   A Valpolicella made from grapes dried and shrivelled on mats in the sun
127.   U.S.A - New York
128.   1385
129.   Veneto
130.   White

WINES OF ITALY – Part 2
131.   Prosecco
132.   Lazio
133.   Orvieto
134.   A Black Rooster/Cockerel
135.   Borgogno Barolo (1761)
136.   Lake Garda
137.   Barolo
138.   Alto Adige
139.   Est!, Est!!, Est!!!
140.   Was Prosecco, new name is Glera

MATCH FAMOUS ITALIAN WINES WITH THEIR DOC AREAS
141.   Frascati   Roma/Lazio
142.   Barolo   Piedmont
143.   Orvieto   Umbria
144.   Greco di Tufo   Campania
145.   Copertino   Puglia
146.   Chianti   Tuscany
147.   Valpolicella   Veneto
148.   Rosso Piceno   Le Marche

| 149. | Vermentino di Gallura | Sardinia |
| 150. | Etna Rosso | Sicily |

ANAGRAMS – ITALY
Italian Grape Varieties
151. Barbera
152. Prosecco
153. Dolcetto
154. Vermentino
155. Montepulciano

Italian Wines
156. Barolo
157. Frascati
158. Barbaresco
159. Chianti
160. Gattinara

WINES OF SPAIN – Part 1
161. Tempranillo
162. Cava
163. False
164. True
165. Red
166. Barcelona or Tarragona
167. Galicia (Rias Baixas)
168. Verdejo
169. Garnacha
170. Ribera del Duero

WINES OF SPAIN – Part 2
171. La Mancha
172. Rioja
173. Fino or Manzanilla
174. 15%
175. Priorat
176. Penedes
177. Marques de Riscal

178.   Freixenet
179.   Emporda (on the Costa Brava)
180.   The Solera System

ANAGRAMS – SPAIN
Spanish Grape Varieties
181.   Tempranillo
182.   Albarino
183.   Carinena
184.   Monastrell
185.   Parellada
Spanish Wine Regions
186.   Priorat
187.   Ribera del Duero
188.   Penedes
189.   Rias Baixas
190.   Somontano

WINES OF NEW ZEALAND – Part 1
191.   Sauvignon Blanc
192.   Nelson
193.   False (in Canterbury)
194.   Central Otago
195.   Canterbury
196.   Gruner Veltliner
197.   Sauvignon Blanc
198.   South Island
199.   LVMH (Louis Vuitton Moet Hennessy)
200.   Hawkes Bay

WINES OF NEW ZEALAND – Part 2
201.   Marlborough
202.   Two Paddocks
203.   Pernod Ricard
204.   1.5% and growing
205   30 million cases
206.   700

207.	Central Otago
208.	USA
209.	75%
210.	Villa Maria

ANAGRAMS – NEW ZEALAND
New Zealand Wine Regions
211.	Marlborough
212.	Gisborne
213.	Hawkes Bay
214.	Auckland
215.	Central Otago

New Zealand Wine Producers
216.	Villa Maria
217.	Ata Rangi
218.	Stonyridge
219.	Jackson Estate
220.	Felton Road

WINES OF CHILE
221.	Bio Bio
222.	Cabernet Sauvignon
223.	Carmenere
224.	Miguel Torres
225.	Chateau Lafite Rothschild
226.	Maipo
227.	340
228.	Not grafted onto North American root stock/Phylloxera free
229.	4th in 2015
230.	Concha y Toro

WINES OF ARGENTINA
231.	Malbec
232.	March/April
233.	Red
234.	1557

235. Mendoza
236. Bodegas Weinert
237. Norton
238. Torrontes
239. 900
240. Colome

ANAGRAMS – SOUTH AMERICA
South American Grape Varieties
241. Carmenere
242. Torrontes
243. Bonarda
244. Trebbiano
245. Tannat

Argentinian and Chilean Wine Regions
246. Patagonia
247. Central Valley
248. San Antonio
249. Salta
250. Maule

WINES OF GERMANY – Part 1
251. Qualitatswein mit Pradikat
252. Eiswein/Ice Wine
253. Auslese
254. Dry
255. Pinot Noir
256. Trockenbeerenauslese
257. The Saar and the Ruwer
258. Baden
259. Bocksbeutel
260. Ahr, Baden, Wurttemberg

WINES OF GERMANY – Part 2
261. USA
262. 35%
263. Kabinett

ANAGRAMS – GERMANY
German Grape Varieties
German Wine Towns

WINES OF U.S.A. – CALIFORNIA – Part 1

WINES OF U.S.A. – CALIFORNIA – Part 2

293. E & J Gallo
294. Moet & Chandon, Mumm, Roederer, Taittinger
295. Santa Barbara
296. Mendocino County
297. 5%
298. 4th largest (after France, Italy, Spain)
299. Starboard
300. Kendal Jackson Chardonnay

ANAGRAMS – USA, CALIFORNIA
Californian Wine Valleys
301. Santa Clara
302. Sonoma
303. Edna
304. Santa Ynez
305. Dry Creek
Californian Wine Producers
306. Beringer
307. Bonny Doone
308. Stags Leap
309. Au Bon Climat
310. Chateau Montelena

WINES OF PORTUGAL
311. Setubal
312. Douro Valley, Pico Island
313. Vinho Verde
314. 30
315. Cliff Richard
316. Mateus Rose
317. Espumante
318. Madeira
319. Colares
320. Kopke

ANAGRAMS – PORTUGAL
Port Producers
321. Quinta da Noval
322. Cockburn
323. Taylors
324. Fonseca
325. Sandeman

Portuguese DOC Wines
326. Bucelas
327. Douro
328. Bairrada
329. Setubal
330. Dao

WINES OF SOUTH AFRICA
331. 55%
332. K W V (Koöperatieve Wijnbouwers Vereniging van Zuid-Afrika Bpkt)
333. Klein Constantia
334. Hamilton Russell
335. The UK
336. Ernie Els
337. Pinotage
338. Goats do Roam
339. Vergelegen
340. Chenin Blanc

ANAGRAMS – SOUTH AFRICA
South African Wine Regions
341. Constantia
342. Stellenbosch
343. Franshhoek
344 Robertson
345. Walker Bay

South African Wine Producers
346. Beyerskloof
347. Rustenberg

348. Meerlust
349. Steenberg
350. Thelema

WINES OF AUSTRALIA – Part 1
351. Wyndham Estate
352. USA
353. Shiraz
354. Penfolds Grange
355. Tasmania
356. Wolf Blass
357. Tarrango
358. South Australia
359. Len Evans
360. Leeuwin Estate

WINES OF AUSTRALIA – Part 2
361. China
362. Moet & Chandon
363. Approximately 2,500 wineries are currently operating
364. Barossa Valley
365. Chardonnay
366. 1,500 million bottles
367. James Busby
368. Fosters
369. Pinot Noir
370. James Halliday

ANAGRAMS – AUSTRALIA
Australian Wine Regions
371. Adelaide Hills
372. Coonawarra
373. Geelong
374. Rutherglen
375. Riverland
Australian Wine Producers
376. Stonier

377. Wolf Blass
378. Brokenwood
379. Yalumba
380. Petaluma

WINES OF ENGLAND
381. Nyetimber
382. 5 million
383. Nyetimber
384. Cornwall
385. Stanlake Park
386. York
387. Three Choirs
388. 10%
389. 22 (grown commercially)
390. 43AD (almost as soon as the Romans arrived)

ANAGRAMS – ENGLAND
English Wine Producers
391. Denbies
392. Breaky Bottom
393. Nyetimber
394. Camel Valley
395. Three Choirs
English Wine Grape Varieties
396. Bacchus
397. Schonburger
398. Dornfelder
399. Seyval Blanc
400. Rondo

AUSTRIA/HUNGARY/GREECE
401. Gruner Veltliner
402. Red
403. 25%
404. Burgenland (near to Lake Neusiedl)
405. Bikaver (Egri Bikaver from Eger and Bikaver from Szekszard)

406. Tokaji
407. Lake Balaton
408. Santorini
409. Boutari (voted one of the top 10 wineries in the world)
410. Retsina (now under 10% of all Greek Wines)

ANAGRAMS – AUSTRIA
Austrian Wine Regions
411. Wien
412. Kremstal
413. Burgenland
414. Wagram
415. Kamptal
Austrian Grape Varieties
416. Gruner Veltliner
417. Blaufrankisch
418. Riesling
419. St Laurent
420. Zweigelt

HISTORY OF WINE
421. 5k–6k BC
422. Iran
423. 17th Century
424. 16th Century
425. The 1930's (1935)
426. 1982
427. 1662
428. Bordeaux reds and Sherry
429. Le Pin in Pomerol
430. In France in the 1960's

WINE GROWING AND WINE MAKING
431. Jan/Feb
432. 25 to 30 years (Vieilles Vignes from then on, more minerality and intensity)
433. The influence a plot of land has on the wine it produces (made up of climate, soil type and topography)

434.   16C – 21C

435.   To remove sediment. (Called fining, also done with many other products)

436.   The pre-fermented juice of red or white grapes which also contains the skins, seeds, and stems. (Usually only juice is used in the fermentation of white wines)

437.   600 on average for 750ml bottles

438.   Troncais – the slowest growing and tightest growing oak, most costly barrels

439.   2 years minimum in oak (and then 3 years minimum in bottle before sale)

440.   300 standard bottles

WINE TASTING

441.   10,000 plus

442.   Sweet, sour, salt, bitter

443.   To ensure it is fault free and at the right temperature

444.   Sauvignon Blanc

445.   It is TCA tainted from cork fault, and smells musty (wet cardboard, old socks)

446.   Robert Parker

447.   Cabernet Sauvignon

448.   High alcohol content (it's glycerine which is related to viscosity & alcohol)

449.   Pinot Noir

450.   The lingering taste, sense and perception of the wine after swallowing it

FAMOUS PEOPLE/FAMOUS WINES – Part 1

451.   Bollinger

452.   Chianti Ruffino

453.   F. Scott Fitzgerald in The Great Gatsby

454.   Pol Roger (P R now have a special Churchill Cuvee)

455.   Pinot Noir

456.   Vintage Dom Perignon from Moet & Chandon

457.   Geoffrey Chaucer

458.   £2million

459.   Napoleon Bonaparte

460.   Ridgeview (Rosé)

FAMOUS PEOPLE/FAMOUS WINES – Part 2

461.   Sam Neill (Two Paddocks Vineyard)

462.   Waitrose (has the Royal Warrant)

463.   Keith Floyd

464.   Chateau Lafite (1787 from Thomas Jefferson's collection)

465.   Mateus Rosé

466.   Chateau d'Yquem

467.   Graham Beck's (from South Africa)

468.   Bordeaux (Chateau Bauduc)

469.   Chateau Canon (1st Class growth from St Emilion)

470.   Madonna's (real name is Madonna Louise Veronica
        Ciccone)

FAMOUS WINE QUOTES – Part 1

471.   On his first sip of Champagne, which he had just invented

472.   Shakespeare (in As You Like it)

473.   Charles Dickens

474.   Alexander Fleming (the inventor of Penicillin)

475.   Geoffrey Chaucer

476.   Napoleon Bonaparte

477.   W. C. Fields

478.   Benjamin Franklin

479.   Humphrey Bogart (in Casablanca as Rick Blaine to Ingrid
        Bergman as Ilsa Lund)

480.   Martin Luther

FAMOUS WINE QUOTES – Part 2

481.   The Bible (Book of Ecclesiastes)

482.   James Joyce

483.   Anonymous (no one knows)

484.   Thomas Jefferson

485.   Samuel Johnson

486.   Sideways

487.   Pliny the Elder

488.   Robert Parker

489.   Oliver Reed

490.   Ernest Hemmingway

GENERAL WINE QUESTIONS – Finale

491.   Lafite-Rothschild, Latour, Margaux, Mouton-Rothschild, Haut-Brion

492.   True

493.   Green

494.   Any of these

495.   Brown

496.   False

497.   Sussex

498.   Sauternes or Barsac

499.   False

500.   Pinot Blanc

About the Authors:

Roddy Button

Roddy started his career working for a centuries-old wine company in Bristol. His responsibilities included the enjoyable task of decanting and tasting wines from the 'Directors Bin', some of which dated back to the late 19th century.

When the business was taken over by a large wine and spirit company, Roddy moved to London to work on the marketing and advertising of various wine and spirit products.

Having successfully completed all the Wine and Spirit Education Trust's exam courses, right through to Diploma, Roddy is now an AIWS, Associate member of the Institute of Wines and Spirits.

Roddy is passionate about wine and, along with Mike Oliver, his co-author of 'The Wine Quiz Book' and 'Wine: 101 Truths, Myths and Legends', regularly attends international wine tastings in London, as well as travelling every year to different wine regions to meet producers and taste their wines.

Mike Oliver

Mike's interest in wine began at university where he was a member of the wine tasting team, a role that sparked a lifelong involvement in the wine trade.

During his career, Mike has advertised many international brands of wines and spirits, a position which has regularly brought him into close contact with international wine producers.

He frequently takes part in trade and consumer wine tastings in London and, on one occasion, narrowly lost out on the Wine Taster of the Year award to well-known wine expert Oz Clarke. Mike's passion for wine has made him an enthusiastic collector of both new and antique wine books.

With his co-author of 'The Wine Quiz Book' and 'Wine: 101 Truths, Myths and Legends', Roddy Button, Mike makes regular trips abroad to visit wine regions and meet wine makers, from local farmers to internationally celebrated estates and families.

www.apexpublishing.co.uk

CPSIA information can be obtained
at www.ICGtesting.com
Printed in the USA
BVHW031521080719
552773BV00010B/205/P